Pendulum Dowsing

Discover the Secrets of Dowsing with Your Pendulum

a
Step by Step Guide
by Dr. Shé D'Montford

Pendulum Dowsing
Discover the Secrets of Dowsing with Your Pendulum

Dowsing is a natural ability that everybody has, once shown how simple it is, you will be able to ask the pendulum revealing questions about yourself and others. Once you have developed your dowsing abilities you will find that the pendulum will become part of your everyday life.

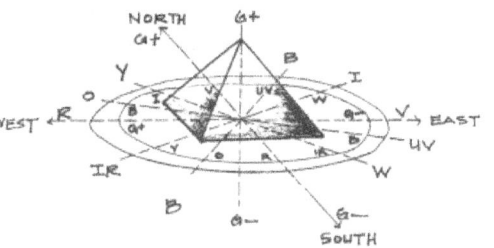

Dowsing - sometimes referred to as water witching or divining is an ancient technique used to sense things that concealed from plain sight. Traditionally, it was used to uncover water sources. At one time it was the only way to find if you had water on your land. Water divining is still used today with stunning results. Dowsing has been used for centuries. The ancient Egyptians were master dowsers; pendulums have been found in the tombs of their high priests. More recently, dowsing has been used by U.S Marines in Vietnam to locate underground mines and tunnels. French physicians used dowsing to help them make a diagnosis, known as radiethesia. The practice of dowsing, either by pendulum or rod, is noted before the time of Queen Cleopatra, who's own advisors used them extensively. You don't have to use your pendulum to find water for it has so many other uses, search for precious stones or oxides and even missing persons. You can dowse to find lost items, or to see if you have allergies to certain foods. Healers use a Pendulum to find causes for illness in their patients; engineers locate errors on drawings; computer experts find errors in computer code; gold and oil deposits are found; buried treasure and ancient artefacts are located; water, electric, and telephone utilities use dowsing to find their lines. You can contact animals and vegetation. Dowsing has been used in many places to increase food crops by helping plants grow, keeping bugs away, and even putting a protective field around them to prevent diseases. There are many other uses of Dowsing that are not covered here. You can also use dowsing as an aid to help you make those all-important decisions. However, for those who possess a spiritual aptitude, it can be used to answer very specific questions.

The Science Behind Dowsing

Dowsing is intuition technology. Dowsing tools include `L' shaped metal rods, `Y' shaped wooden rods, and a weight on the end of a length of string called a Pendulum. These simple tool can be used as receivers in a similar way that a an old wire, a rusty razor blade and the graphite from a pencil, is a simple technology that can pick up radio signals (a crystal radio). Humans are a much more sensitive receiver than a simple crystal radio set. We are all able to sense so many things including electro-magnetic energy not visible to the naked eye. All things give off energetic radiation. A pendulum receives information from the vibrations and energy waves emitted by people, places, thoughts and things, Our own senses can feel and measure these energies. The pendulum becomes our communication device between conscious and subconscious. Through unconsciously manoeuvring a dowsing rod or pendulum we use this skill that is not present in our conscious brains. Scientists refer to this as

"The Ideomotor Effect". When a conscious mind is in a clear receptive state and focused upon a carefully worded question it opens a communications channel that answers by giving subconscious muscular impulses which which are exaggerated and amplified by the use of the simple tool. This bypasses the conscious, thinking mind, which tends to block intuition.

However, becoming an "expert" dowser is not as simple as it seems. It needs practise, over time to improve and refine the understanding of the process that you are going through and to give it accurate meaning. Though you may experience some beginners success your skills will improve and get better with practise. Once you have reached a level of competence keeping your hand in, is important as even as an expert may lose your skills if they do not keep on practicing. Learning to Dowse is like learning to read. Once you have started, you can apply it to many fields.

a) Dowsing with Pendulums
Dowsing may be conducted by attaching a metal, crystal or stone weight to a chain or string. In my experience conductive crystals on a string work the best. Pendulum dowsing is most useful for Yes/No investigations, hovering the weight above a diagram of options, can give you surprisingly accurate results.

b) Dowsing with rods
Find a Y-shaped piece of branch, holding the split ends as pictured. Experts believe that the best wood for this purpose is either Willow or Hazel - the lighter nature of the material is more suited to sensing underground water or metal vapours.

A Step-by-Step Guide for the Open Minded

Prepare Yourself

To unlock your inner potential, it's important that you are physically relaxed. In initiating dowsing, you must enter with a peaceful state of mind, not concentrating on the pendulum so much as focusing on the answers you have within yourself. A minute or two of controlled breathing, closed eyes and soothing thoughts, or even meditation will help to distance you from your worldly concerns. Beginning with Shé´D'Montford's ZiGi meditation is the best as it opens your 3rd eye and stills the mind to a clear calm pool of reflection. This is a time to tune into your spiritual core, not be distracted by your 'head' thoughts. Any thoughts that arise, acknowledge them and push the to one side to wait until your work is finished.

Calibrate Your Dowsing Tool

After acquiring a pendulum, whether by purchasing, or crafting one yourself, you must charge it. It is important to note not to let another person handle your pendulum, as this will interrupt your own energy. Hold your dowsing tool out before you and let your mind rest on your question or the object or person you seek. Allow your mind to become the clear calm pool of reflection that will reflect the answers you seek. If you wish to find something begin by visualising the path to your desired goal before you and let the tool move as your subconscious dictates. If you are truly attuned to the psychic energies, the tool will quiver and turn almost imperceptibly towards your destination or the answers on the diagram.

Turning Your Pendulum

It is important to get the right length string for the length of your fore arm. This is called turning your pendulum.

Hold the string between your thumb and first finger of your hand, and slowly let the string out. If you find this difficult, wrap the string around a pencil first; but be sure to hold the string (on the pencil) between your thumb and first finger. Start with about 5cm (2 inches) of string between your finger and the pendulum weight. Let the string out a little at a time, and soon your Pendulum will start to make a circle; continue to let out the string slowly, and your Pendulum will go back to swinging again; let out more string until your Pendulum starts making a circle again - note that this circle is much larger than the first circle. Then you have found the correct place to hold the string of your Pendulum. If you are very sensitive, your Pendulum may make very large circles all the time when using this length; if this is so, then use the shorter length - when your Pendulum first started to make a circle. Mark this the ' holding point ' by making a simple slip knot in the string.

Do not be disheartened if you have little or no results the first time you attempt dowsing - it is an ancient and mystical technique that has taken hundreds of years to perfect. Just enjoy the experience and don't try... just let things be as they should.

1. Take 3 single embroidery strands, 30cm or 12" long, and thread them through your pendulum.
2. Hold the string or chain between your thumb and forefinger, about 7&1/2 cm or 3" from the weight, or mass, being used
3. Touch the nose of the pendulum to the central mark on the diagram then lift it away slowly.
4. Hold the pendulum only about 1cm above the dowsing diagram in the middle of this booklet, holding

it as immobile as I could. Keeping your elbow firmly down on the table, as pictured, will help prevent nervous or accidental wiggles. First of all, just focus on keeping it still. eventually it will begin to move without your conscious intention.

5. Place your other elbow against the side of your body, with the hand in front of you, palm upwards, pointing out in front of your body to the side and level with your waist.

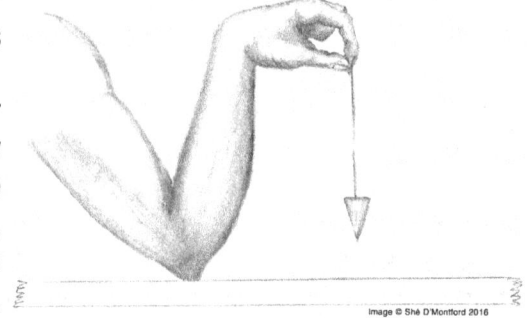

6. You must not try to make your pendulum move in any way.
7. You will find that your pendulum will swing variously around in a circle, or back and forth (either head-tail or side-side). This swinging motion is known as amplitude. Test which way is "Yes" and which way is "No" by asking your pendulum some test questions that you all ready know the answers to. On the diagram the vertical axis is "Yes" and the horizontal axis is "No."
8. You can also strengthen your communication with your pendulum by holding your pendulum over the clockwise circle, and asking it to move in a clockwise direction; if it does not move the first time, try again later. Keep at this until it moves. Do not make it move, just wait for your Pendulum to move on its own! This

9. is very important, since you are trying to confirm that the signal is understood. Repeat for the anti-clockwise circle. Then in straight lines. This is an important step as it establishes strong communication between you and your pendulum. You can use this skill to find lost and stolen items, read messages, seek treasure, and find your way home, by asking it to swing in that direction.
10. Circling usually happens around something that the energy wants to draw your attention to. Pain, is a universal billboard and you will find that sessions will often begin with the pendulum circling around an area on the body part of the diagram that reflects in your, or the person you are dowsing for, body that is in pain. This is a clear indication that you have come 'on-line' with these subtle energies. Just acknowledge to the universe that you have got the message and that you are ready to move on so that you can clearly pick up the answers to you questions.
11. Alternatively, the axis may change after your initial check and the swing of the pendulum will point to the answer, a number or begin spelling out a word like a Ouija board.
12. This is how it works most often. It is sensible to check which way the energy is working that way for you. We all have off days or days where we feel scrambled. Just as when we move a transistor radio from place to place the tuning may be slightly different in order to receive a clear transmission. It is good to check to see how it is best for you to 'tune-in'. A test question each time before you begin will demonstrate to you which is the best way to receive the messages on that day. The purpose of programming the amplitude is to achieve maximum accuracy. You are offering mutually

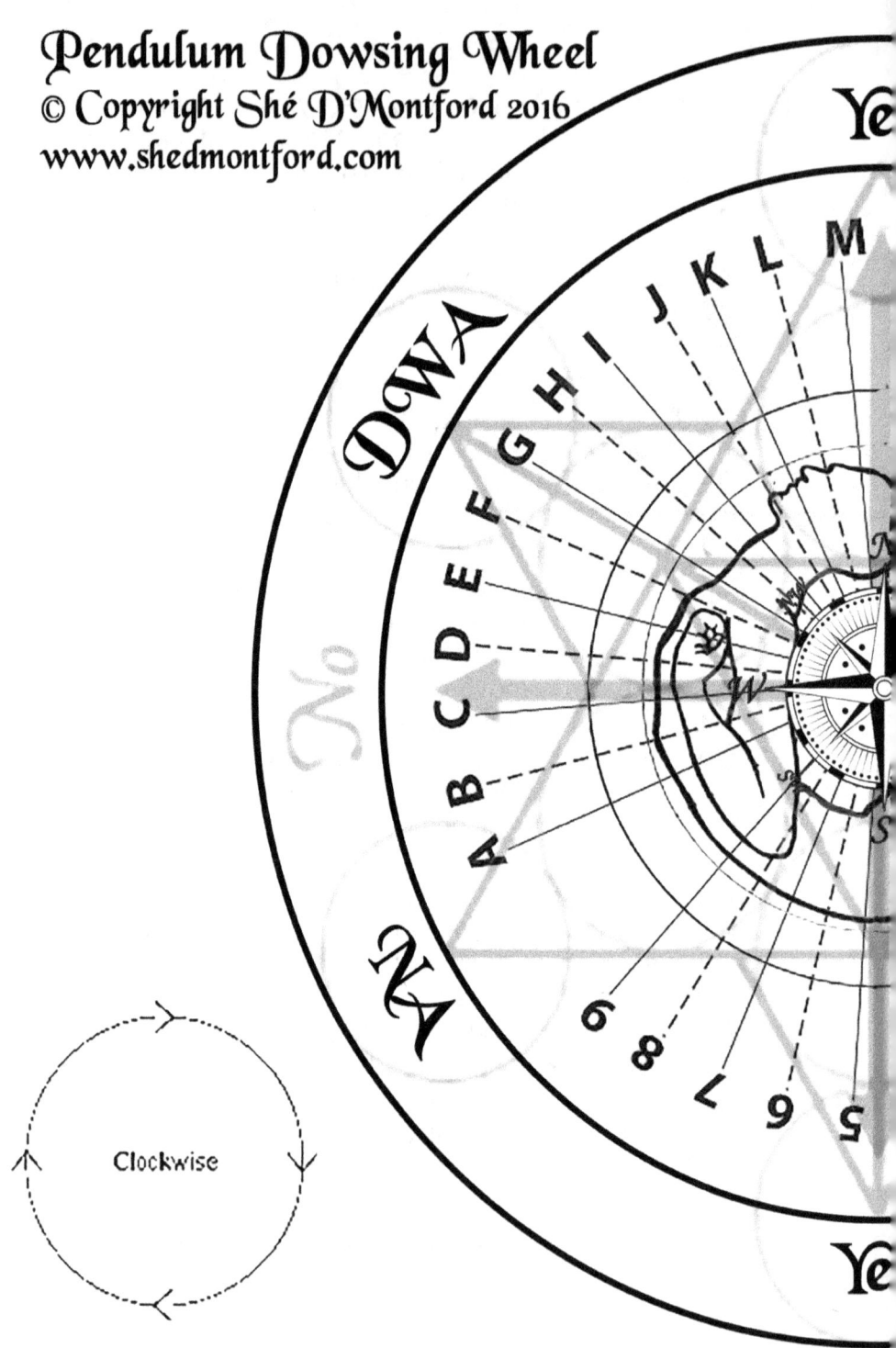

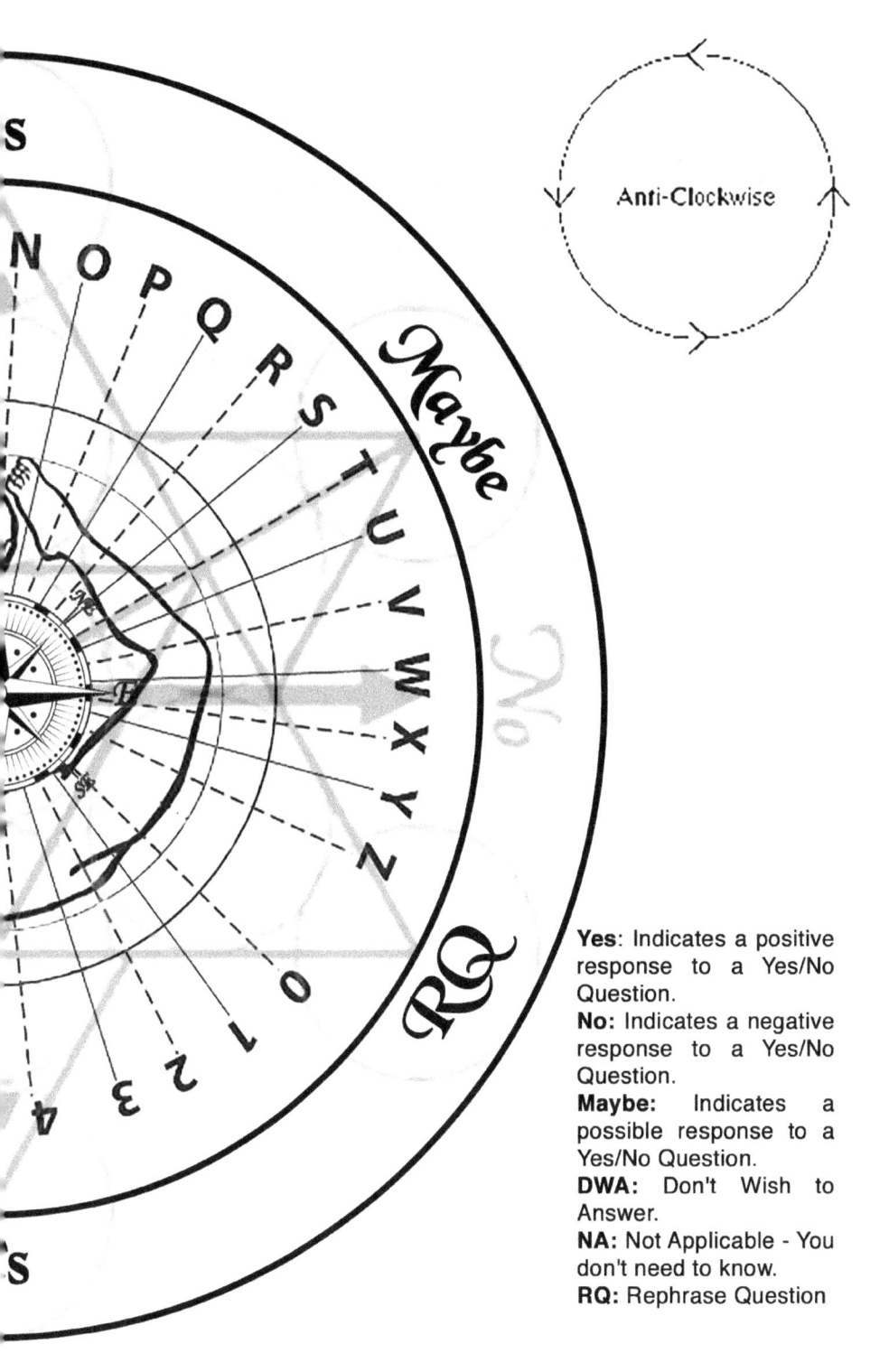

Yes: Indicates a positive response to a Yes/No Question.
No: Indicates a negative response to a Yes/No Question.
Maybe: Indicates a possible response to a Yes/No Question.
DWA: Don't Wish to Answer.
NA: Not Applicable - You don't need to know.
RQ: Rephrase Question

acceptable, pre-established agreements and understandings about words and what is meant by different pendulum movements. Practice daily until you are confident in different movements and their meaning. Then you will be ready to start utilizing your pendulum.
13. You can also use it to assess problems in your own body, as well as broadening your intuition and knowledge of myself.
14. When seeking information from dowsing, as I stated previously, talk to the pendulum as if it were a person. This will direct the energies to the pendulum, and not you. This frees your mind to concentrate on the action not the answers.
15. Stay away from microwave frequency electrical equipment while dowsingle switch of mobile phones/devices, TVs, internet, wifi and microwave ovens if you can. This will allow for greater accuracy and clarity. .

Accurate & Appropriate Questions

There are some very important rules about the questions that you ask.
- even if it is not what you intended The questions you ask must be clear in order for them to be accurate. For instance, if you are thinking about eating more ice cream the question "Is it OK?" is NOT clear - rather ask "Is it OK for me to eat more ice cream now ?"
It is best to ask only question that can be answered with a Yes or No when you are beginning. Example; If somebody told you a story, asking ` Is the story true ?' may not work, because some of it may be true, and some of it may not be true. So you must ask about the part of the story that you think may be untrue.

There are appropriate and non-appropriate types of questions to ask when dowsing. There are some questions which should NOT be asking, especially if the question is not your business! This is why it is very important to ask your pendulum, "May I ask about XXX ?" Appropriate questions are about things that are within your control, or about things your subconscious already has access to. The following are very good questions you may use:
- Making a choice of any kind
- What is best to do in a situation
- Figuring out your true feelings
- Assessing other people and their motives
- Finding causes of physical symptoms
- Determining what foods and vitamins to take

You may have to start with broad questions, then narrow them down.

Inaccurate Answers

The following are causes for incorrect response from the pendulum:

1) Poor communication, or inaccurate phrasing are causes for an incorrect response from your pendulum.
2) Do not be too general. Do not ask "Is my spouse healthy?" Pinpoint the question by asking "Are my husband's eating habits causing his health problems?" Don't ask "Is this water good for me?" Rephrasing this to "Will this water serve my highest and greatest good?'... you are narrowing down the question for a more specific answer.
3) Practice getting accurate answers to things like guessing the cards in a pack, telling dates of coins, or finding non-essential things.

4) Don't confuse getting an answer that you don't want with a wrong answer. At times you may address questions to an animal, a tree, your car or your computer; they will respond to the exact question that you ask, even though it may not be the answer that you wanted. *"Is my understanding of that answer correct ?"* is a good way to check that the question was what you intended, that you have understood the answer, and that the answer given was the correct answer.

With practice and an open mind, you will learn to rely on dowsing to aid you in many aspects of your life.

Bonding With Your Pendulum
A Pendulum can be made from a paper-clip on a hair, a brass weight on a string. Some people their key or a crystal on a metal chain. A combination of inorganic and organic materials has proven the most effective.

If you are using a crystal pendulum, it is easy to bond with the little spirit that inhabits the stone. It will pick you to work with as much as you choose it. First bond together with your Pendulum as a team. Set an intention and working parameters. Communicate to it how important the truth is to you and that you hope to work with it in the spirit of truth. Here is a suggestion for a verbal contract between you and your pendulum:

Hold your pendulum in your non-dominant hand, the hand you will be working with when you hold your pendulum and say:
"I, (your name), the spirit of this Pendulum, declare that all answers derived from our collaboration shall always

be given in the Love of Truth; We promise together to utilise our dowsing collaboration only for the highest good. We ask The Universal Life Force Energies help guide us to the answers that are the best available and are true, that they apply to the present time, and that they be within our range of understanding. "

The Zigi Breath 'will help you be a clear calm pool of reflection for your dowsing and will allow you to start to tangibly experience dowsing as a 3 way collaboration of intelligences. Between you your pendulum and intelligent energy. Remember to keep your conscious awareness at the top of your nose, between your eyebrows, opening the third eye and breathing deeply. Feel your breath with your conscious awareness; exhale, moving your conscious awareness straight back into your head, through your nasal passages, look up with your eyes and open your eyes. Your conscious awareness will expand, and your mind chatter will quieten.

Conclusion

Mastering the art of pendulum dowsing can be rewarding. It is a handy divination tool. it is another tool in your psychic tool box that will be useful to you and your clients. As with all tools, they can lie mouldering in the bottom of your tool box or you can practise with them daily until you gain the ability to become a master trades person and accomplish great things with it.

A Happy Medium Publication For -

Shambhallah Awareness Centre
P.O. Box 3541 Helensvale Town Centre. Q. 4212.

http://www.shambhallah.org

Pendulum Dowsing
a
Step by Step Guide
by Dr. Shé D'Montford

ISBN-13: 978-0-9943477-8-7

© Copyright Rev. Dr. S. D'Montford,
Wednesday April 13, 2016 - Gold Coast. Australia.

All **Rights Reserved.** The information presented is protected under the Berne Convention for the Protection of Literature and Artistic works, under other international conventions and under national laws on copyright and neighbouring rights. Extracts of the information in this book may be reviewed, but not reproduce without express written permission from the publisher. Reproduction or translation of portions of this publication requires explicit, prior authorisation in writing.

Obligatory Disclaimer: Published by Shambhallah Awareness Centre for historical, cultural, educational and entertainment purposes only. No therapeutic value is implied. The primary reason for this publication is entertainment and education about traditional health and spiritual practices. While Shambhallah Awareness Centre has used all reasonable endeavours to ensure the information in this book is as accurate as possible, it gives no warranty or guarantee that the material, information, or publications made accessible by them are fit for any use whatsoever nor does that excuse you from using your common-sense. Shambhallah Awareness Centre and Rev. Dr S. D'Montford accepts no liability or responsibility for any loss or damage whatsoever suffered as a result of direct or indirect use or application of any material, publication or information obtained from them.

Dowsing is a natural ability that everybody has, once shown how simple it is, you will be able to ask the pendulum revealing questions about yourself and others. Once you have developed your dowsing abilities you will find that the pendulum will become part of your everyday life

Discover the Secrets of Dowsing with Your Own Pendulum

Each set contains your own genuine silver chain &
925 SILVER SET GEMSTONE CRYSTAL PENDULUM
carved into the correct traditional shape for pendulum dowsing, so that you can learn correctly and practise the techniques as they are explained to you.

The centre of the book is a
DOWSING CHART
designed by Shé D'Montford, to make your personal dowsing experience easy to gauge.

A Happy Medium Publication For -
Shambhallah Awareness Centre
P.O. Box 3541 Helensvale Town Centre. Q. 4212.

http://www.shambhallah.org

© Copyright Rev. Dr. S. D'Montford,
Wednesday April 13, 2016 - Gold Coast. Australia.

ISBN-13: 978-0-9943477-8-7

www.ingramcontent.com/pod-product-compliance
Lightning Source LLC
Chambersburg PA
CBHW052132010526
44113CB00034B/1906